The Little Pillow Book of Tantra
Inspirations for connected Loving.

Waratah Karleu

Copyright © 2015 Waratah Karleu

Published by the Umber Chrysanthemum
PO Box 1056,
Stirling,
SA 5152.

All rights reserved. No part of this book may be reproduced or transmitted in any form without written permission from the publisher, except by reviewers who may quote brief excerpts in connection with a review.

Cover design by Isabel Kumerz.
Edited by Judi Blaze.
Interior designs by Waratah Karleu.
Layout for publication by Judi Blaze.

ISBN-10:
0994271905
ISBN-13:
978-0-9942719-0-7

With deep appreciation of the lineage of Tantrikas who preceded me, for my teachers and guides, lovers and husband (ex though he may be).

With dedicated gratitude to Pea for opening my heart beyond all others.

Introduction

Tantra is about connection with ourselves; and if we have one, connection with our partner. From there we connect with the higher source for whatever name you may give it. Tantra can be seen as mindfulness in sexuality. We activate our own sexual energy, our life force and we co-activate our partner's; from there a third energy is created that we can use for healing ourselves and others.

However, we need to create the solid ground on which to do this. Trust, connection, openness, vulnerability and love are the requisites which form the basis of intimacy.

We often use sex to avoid intimacy.

This book will guide you through practices to enable deeper intimacy through greater connection with yourself and your beloved.

Take your time, slow down, there is no rush. Feel all of the feelings, the sensations, and the shifts and changes as you explore yourself and your beloved in all of the many ways possible.

Through this practice we balance our energies, coming into harmony with each other. We create more energy in our lives to nurture those around us, and indeed humanity as a whole.

This book, although written from a heterocentric perspective, is just as relevant for all, regardless of any sexual orientation.

"Look past your thoughts, so you may drink the pure nectar of This Moment,"

- Rumi

Terminology

Let's begin with finding a terminology that works for you; that empowers and resonates with you for your lady and man parts.

Within this book I will use the Tantric terminology:

Shiva masculine….yang…hot….extroverted.
Lingam (penis), translates as wand of light.

Shakti…..feminine….yin….cool….introverted.
Yoni (vulva), translates as sacred temple.

However, the Taoist terminology is also divine; jade flute, jade stem or jade emperor for the lingam.

The yoni, the jade temple, jade palace, or cinnabar cave.

For oral sex, playing the jade flute, or on a woman sipping the vast spring (which also pertains to the belief in the elixir of youth from the yoni juices)

One of my favourites for conjuring up erotic imagery is; 'the emperor is at the palace gates'.

Find terminology that works, that speaks of love and loving your sexuality and your genitalia.

Creating the space

Come together with gentleness and awareness, step into another realm away from your everyday, where all argument and anything that doesn't belong in a sacred space is left outside.

Remember when you were first dating and you took the time to make sure that everything was just right to invite your beloved into. This is fundamental; come back to the care and energy you took and bring this back to your relationship.

Make and create a Sacred Space

Create the space through ritual and time scheduling

Ritual can be simple or complex.

Let your intention be your guide.

Alter, Rug, Cushions, Flowers, Candles

Wash your body, clean the room, clear your space, you may choose to wear special clothing, a kimono or symbolic garment, maybe its lingerie.

Set aside time, make a date. For instance, Thursday evening at 8 p.m. for 30 minutes.

Make it manageable and show up.

We schedule the rest of our lives, but somehow we think it is not necessary to do this within our relationships.

When we are in a new relationship we make the time, the dates, the space, but for some reason this fundamental gets swept aside in longer term relationships

Make your agreements

How often, what time, and for how long, then stick to them.

Through integrity, we build trust, the key stone to our opening and connection.

Take turns setting up the space.

Whether it is making a date, running a bath, or choosing what you would like to explore.

Be utterly surprised at how much it is a turn for your lady love when you take the initiative to set up the space.

Taking the time to create the space; creating the care to nurture your relationship.

Ritual creates the space outside of and away from the everyday.

Turn off your phone.

As you would when entering a scared space, because you are, let the everyday fall away.

Altar as an affirmation

Creating an altar

Create an altar as a dedication to your relationship. If you are outside of a relationship, you might want to create an altar to manifest a new partner. Cleanse the altar regularly and each of you brings offerings or gifts to it, such as flowers, or a new candle or crystals. There are no rules for this space, bring what you feel symbolises the nourishment of your love.

When you create your ritual space, use the altar for water and fruit,
light a candle.

You might feel like incorporating each of the elements—such as fire in the form of candles, water to drink, air may be represented by feathers or a leaf blown from a tree, and the earth element with food.

Bring art, poetry and music into your love space.

Building connection

Open your heart through sound.

Take a deep in breath and then let it out fully
AHHHHHHhhhhhh…….sigh and let go of the day
Arrive in your body and feel your heart opening.

Close your eyes and connect with your self firstly. Feel your whole body as you sit, feel your connection with the floor and the earth below, let your whole body relax and become present.

Sit before your beloved and gaze into each other's least dominant eye (if they are right handed it will be their left)

Begin to coordinate your breathing.
When we do this we align our energies……a simple yet powerful daily practice to stay in tune with each other.

Try to be aware of your facial expressions and relax away from them.
Soften your jaw, your eyes, your tongue
let the skin of your face be smooth.

There is nothing to do here but to be with yourself and with your beloved.

This may not be easy initially,
but it becomes more comfortable with practice.

Begin with your eyes open, make your breath audible and find a pace that works for you both.

Continue to breathe and then close your eyes and keep breathing together.

When you are ready, open your eyes and continue breathing together, letting go of tension in your face and body.

The mind may get distracted, watch the distraction, can you let it go and come back to being present?

Honouring each other

Honour the divine masculine/feminine in your partner.

We are Gods and Goddesses here on vacation.

When we are honoured in this way it helps us to rise into the best possible versions of our self.

When we honour our beloved in this way it helps us to see them in their best possible light.

(Try also honouring the sacred masculine within your feminine partner and vice versa, remember we are all part feminine and part masculine. Feel how it feels to be honoured in that way.)

Take turns placing your hand over your partner's heart centre; continue gazing into his eyes, continue connected breathing.

'I honour the divine masculine (or feminine) within you'.

If you are the one receiving this devotion take a moment to feel it, breathe it into your body and then thank your partner with a simple thank you.

When we say thank you we let our partner know we have fully received his or her gift.

Honour the light, the love and the joy in your beloved.

Sharing

Share…How did that feel?….'I felt…….'

Feel how it was for you….be real…if it was uncomfortable say so.

Keep it about you…. 'I felt………..'

As your partner shares, breath it in and respond with thank you, even if it was difficult to hear.

Safety and Trust

Sometimes we may find it difficult to receive love; maybe we find it easier to give. If that's the case, acknowledge it or whatever else comes up. This is about being vulnerable, go gently and with awareness.

Create the space for SAFETY.

This is about being in the now, the present moment with your feelings.

TRUST...

Make trust your muse and guide.

Ask permission and talk about boundaries.

When you finish your session or ritual, close the space.

Honour each other for the sharing.

Blow out the candle.

Yoga

Move your body, breathe, let go of tension.

Be fully alive in your body.

Move your hips, this will get your energy activated.

Let the movement flow up your spine.

Let the breath travel through your body.

The more you can connect with your body on a daily level, the more you will be able to connect with your body and your partner's body within intimacy.

Vagus Nerve

The nerves from the genitals wrap around the coccyx and sacrum, keep these areas open with yoga and stretching.
Sitting cross legged on the floor rather than on a couch at least once a day is a great start.
The vagus nerve has been shown, within positive psychology, to connect the head and the heart.
The vagus nerve also connects with the genitals.
A strong nerve tone has been found in happy people and allows for greater connection with others.
We can maintain the strength of the tone through connecting with others by
eye contact and active listening.

What gives my heart joy?

Share what it is that gives your heart joy.

Take turns sharing 3 things.

Take a few breaths and really come into your heart. You might want to place your hands over your heart, and feel into the things that give your heart joy.

Gazing at your partner you say "Something my heart enjoys is ...."

It doesn't have to be big, something as simple as laying in the sun, walking up a mountain, or a warm sweet cup of tea. Whatever it is that comes to mind.

For the listener, breathe in each one and say thank you. This is your partner sharing her/his heart's joy, feel the privilege of being witness to that sharing. Each time he/she shares, breathe it into your body and then say thank you.

These things may change each time you do this exercise. They also may form the basis of how or where you plan your next date.

Appreciation

This exercise can progress to
3 things I appreciate about you……………..

Breathe…Thank you.

What I appreciate about our relationship
is………………..same process…breathe…thank you….
(give/receive 3 things then swap)

Communication

Communication is a process….keep checking in with each other….How was that for you? Or,

how did that feel? ……………Do you want to keep going?

What I appreciate about our relationship……

What I appreciate about our lovemaking…….

This exercise could lead into;

3 things I would like/appreciate to be/have in our love making……..

The receiver needs to fully receive, breathe it in to your body not just your head
and then say thank you.

Through the process of actively listening we create the safety for the sharing. When we truly feel heard we can open up.

Sharing our vulnerability is such an act of beauty and what we all crave, to fully be seen, heard and loved.

Make sure to share after the process………What I felt…… or 'What I discovered……

Shiva and Shakti

Shiva and Shakti….Celestial consorts…when they came together their dance created the universe.

The masculine essence or **Shiva** energy is presence and awareness. He is unchanging, vast, empty and still. He is the mountain energy, he is depth and integrity. Like the banks of the river, he holds the energy. He is clarity, purpose and vision. He is dependable and detached from emotion.

Shiva is the energy when fear comes up that allows us to detach, de-identify and observe.

The space that knows I am not the emotion, allows us to transcend the emotion.

Shiva, the masculine principal is freedom.

Shakti, the feminine aspect is aliveness, juiciness, creativity, fertility, lusciousness and change.

She is the cycle of the moon, of women, of the tides and of the seasons.

She is connection, relationship, birthing and sustaining.

She is the cool breeze and the tornado.

The changing face of the Goddess in all her emotions and guises.

She is death; she destroys what doesn't serve life.

Where Shiva is awareness, Shakti is everything else.

We each to a greater or lesser extent have both of these qualities to our being. We need to call on them at different times to be able to stand in our awareness and presence, and to be able to move and flow with change, with emotion, with our creativity and aliveness. Become aware of how each of these aspects operate within your life, and how you can call upon the qualities at different times.

Love can be a sacred experience.

Breathing together, eye connection and devotion.

We are God's and Goddesses here on vacation.

The eternal dance of Shiva and Shakti.

Look for the pleasure.

Affirm the pleasure.

Mindfulness; to be in the moment with the pleasure.

Permission

Boundaries and Agreements

In addition to the boundaries and agreements I spoke of within creating the space, we need to create known and agreed upon boundaries within our sexuality. For instance, no always means no, and that no can happen anywhere along the line, even if what was previously agreed upon was a yes.

Sometimes we go along with sexual activities because we don't feel we have the power to say no and be respected. You don't want to create these further layers into your relationship; there is enough to heal without adding more. It will shut down trust, thereby shutting down intimacy, connection and inevitably love.

Practice not only saying no, but also hearing no, and for that to be ok.

Watch the feelings that come up as you say no or you hear it.

Hearing no and saying yes

Sit opposite each other and choose who will go first.
Arrive together and find each other's gaze, spend a moment softening
into yourself and your partner.
Be fully present.
The person to go first will ask if he/she can touch a certain part of your body.
It might be your shoulder or your face, or whatever.
Partner 2 will say yes or no.
Partner 1 will breath that in and say thank you, and then either touch that part or not depending on the response.
Repeat this 5 times.
Partner 2 you will say 'yes' 2-3 times and 'no' 2-3 times.
Each time Partner 1 hear's the response to their question breathe this answer in and say thank you.
The important thing is to practice saying and hearing both yes and no. So even if you are ok with your hair being touched, practice saying no. How does that feel to say it, and how does it feel to hear it?

For me personally I feel a greater sense of openness and opening when given the choice to say yes or no. I don't feel the potential pressure to go where I might not want if the boundaries are not clear, therefore closing to any possibility.

Have a discussion about how that felt for both of you. Swap places and repeat the exercise, finish again with a discussion.

How did that feel for you? Be honest.

Sacred Chalice mediation.

For the Shakti's.

Either sitting or standing, rub your hands together activating the heart centre and then place them over your ovaries and womb, your sexual centre, and send love there.
Allow any feelings to come up and keep directing love and acceptance for all that has happened, the babies that have been born and those that haven't been. The abuse from the times you made love when you didn't want to, through to deeper transgressions.
The cycles that your womb has been through and those yet to come.
This is the seat of your power, the second energy centre or chakra is about sex,
money and power.
Begin swirling your pelvic bowl.
Make it slow and sensual.

Imagine you are swirling a brandy balloon with an ancient elixir; the colour of deep amber, a rich earth orange.

Keep swirling your hips, the movements can be as big or small, fast or slow as you like, and keep sending love, acceptance, compassion, healing.

Let the energy build, this is your energy.

Just as if you were swirling a brandy balloon with an aged cognac, the vapours of that elixir would begin to rise, allow those vapours to rise in your body.

As you breathe in, let them come up to your heart, they may even rise to the crown of your head.

As you breathe them out, infuse your whole body/being.

You can begin to engage the PC muscle, squeezing as you inhale, releasing as you exhale.

Draw the energy up from your pelvis and genitals and into your whole body.

This practice could be a morning meditation or an evening ritual with burning candles
and soft sensual music.

You can embody this technique when self pleasuring and when making love.

Get into your heart.

How much love do you feel?

Open your eyes, have eye contact.

Breathe.

Hmmmm.

Give up on performance and make love.

Stop, say something you appreciate about your partner,
watch it turn her on.
These practices can be incorporated into your love
making,
they don't have to be stand-alone practices.

Stay present in the now

you will feel like you are making love to existence

itself.

You are in the presence of a Goddess.

Feel like you are entering a temple.

You are in the presence of a God.

Honour and adore him as such.

Then go wild!

Osho.

Shakti, the feminine, is movement whether it is of the body or the emotions.
It can be a beautiful thing for men to learn to stay present and be potent in that presence.
Allow the storm to pass, stay present.
That is your gift.
Women need to feel safe, to trust, to open; and for men to be uncollapsable.

We all, both men and women in hetero or same sex couplings, move between the Shiva and Shakti, the feminine and the masculine, presence and movement. Watch the dance, a balance of the two is needed. If you are both in your Shiva, the relationship can get very standoffish and cool, if you are both in your Shakti, there may be much arguing and volatility.

Yin and Yang

Women's sexuality is yin, it is cool and watery and needs to be warmed slowly and attentively, a blast of heat does not suffice.
Some women's yin needs more heating than others.
You can keep her from going too cold with daily devotions of eye gazing and connected breathing.
Depending on how her cup of love is filled, it may be your presence, gifts, a beautiful text, or words of appreciation that will keep her yin essence warmed.
Shiva, the masculine element, is hot and fiery. It is easy for his heat to burn up and consume itself.
The yin is used to cool the yang, the yang to warm the yin bringing balance and harmony.

The Yoni is yin, it is introverted and cool. A woman's heart is yang, it is extroverted and out there in the world. The Lingam is yang, it is extroverted and wants to be out there in the world. A man's heart is yin, it is introverted and cool.

We can use the heat of the yang to warm the yin, helping men to feel safe to open their hearts, and for women to feel safe to open her yoni.

This can be done on an individual level or we can do it together by placing one hand to the heart and one to the lingam or yoni, and breathing together. As you breathe, direct the energy from the yang to the yin.

PC Muscle

PC muscle…love muscle….Pubic coccyx muscle.

The PC muscle is what you use when you stop peeing midstream. Begin to strengthen this muscle by squeezing/ releasing repeatedly 20x 3-5 times a day. Sitting in your car/in the office/ standing in a queue. No one can see, no one will know, but you will be building your energy, increasing blood supply, toning your pelvic floor and for the guys, massaging your prostrate. All of which is so very important for your sexual health.

This muscle will allow you to draw energy up away from the genitals, which can help with guys being able to delay ejaculation and eventually have whole body orgasms. For women it will aid in increasing sensate awareness, building more energy and sensation, and allow this to move into the whole body, in addition to the many benefits of maintaining strength to the pelvic floor.

Moving energy

Add the drawing up of the PC muscle to your eye gazing and connected breathing.
As you breathe in, squeeze. As you breath out let go.
Breathe the energy up to your heart as you breathe in, and as you breathe out, let it flow through your body
If you can't feel the energy you can visualise it as a ball of light moving in your body.
You might like to breathe it up to the crown of your head.
You will probably notice that there is a rocking of the pelvis as you do this, incorporate that into your love making as you draw the energy away from the genitals and into your body.
The Microcosmic orbit travels from the genitals along the perineum, up the back of the body to the crown of the head with the inhalation, and then down the front of the body with the exhalation,
resting in the lower pelvis.
Keep the tongue lightly pressed to the roof of your mouth to complete the circuit.
This can be practiced on you own or with your partner.

Play around with moving the energy.

One of you can draw it to your heart and direct it to the other's heart,
so one gives and the other receives and then swap
Use your hands to indicate where you are directing the energy.
As soon as we start talking we can get into our heads and out of the experience.

Ask permission to place your hand on his/her heart and then the other on her yoni/ his lingam.

Take turns rather than doing it together, at least to begin with. This exercise can help to direct the energy from the genitals to the heart to bring a connection there.

There is also a lot of erotic charge and a great way of building energy, and we help to warm the yin space. Sometimes people have difficulty visualising or feeling energy.

By using the gentle hand pressure this may make it easier.

Yab Yum

The woman sits on your lap facing you with legs wrapped around your waist.

You can be clothed or not with your genitals touching.

Begin with eye contact and connect your breathing and then incorporate moving your energy.

U Shape Breath

Breathe in from your yoni to your heart, breathe out from your heart to your yoni.
He then breathes in from his lingam to his heart and out from heart to lingam.
Continue in this way, letting the energy build and directing it from one to the other.
Hold each other, feel the bliss.

Self pleasuring for longevity
Self pleasuring to increase longevity for men, and overcoming rapid ejaculation.

As stated before, strengthening your PC muscle is good for all sorts of things. When the PC muscle is strong and with practice, you can use it to injaculate (you get to orgasm and retain your life force energy, and your erection, yes multiple orgasms are possible for you too). According to one Taoist scholar, 30% of our nutritional intake is used for our reproductive health, so what you lose today will be made up with tomorrow's intake, rather than building more energy. Within the yogic philosophy it's known as Bramacharya, where we honour and preserve our life force energy, through the foods we eat, the air we breathe, water we drink, and our sexual conduct.

The way to practice is to begin on your own when self pleasuring/masturbating.

Firstly, you want to create the space for this ritual. Turn your phone off, door locked or a sign on the door. You want to be completely comfortable and feel the safety to explore this fully with no distractions.

Play around with touching your body all over and really get into the sense of pleasure that can be derived from that (this may feel uncomfortable at first as nowhere are we taught to be able to fully give to ourselves the pleasure we crave from others).
You may begin to discover areas that you didn't even imagine were pleasurable.
Slow down, touch your face softly, touch your chest, you belly.
Drink in the sensation.
Find out how you like to be touched, where you liked to be touched, the pressure, and speed that you enjoy. This will make it easier for you to be able to direct your partner.
Allow yourself to become more in touch with your whole body as a sensate being.

Sensitise your body to touch and pleasure.

So much of the learning for male sexuality is genitally focused,
expand your repertoire of sensuality.
You want your whole body and your mind to be present in each unfolding moment.

Sensuality for the sake of sensuality. Let go of chasing the orgasm.

This is mindfulness in action and it might require some unlearning to begin with.

When you are ready to stroke your lingam, slow down and be present with each movement and each and every new sensation.

Keep breathing, deep rhythmical breaths. The moment you stop breathing, the tension starts to build in your body.

Bring yourself to about 20% arousal.

When you are there, hold your lingam with one hand, squeeze the PC muscle and gently sweep your other hand up your torso to your heart as you breathe in. As you breathe out, let go of any tension including the PC muscle, but also in your butt, your face, jaws, eyes, tongue.
You want to become aware of your body as it tightens, as well as your mind and its story. Can you let it go and be in the moment?

Allow your arousal to subside to 10%.

Listen to your mind, it might have a story around performance or hurrying. Sometimes this can be born form our earliest sexual pleasuring experiences. Watch the thoughts and let them go, be completely present to the moment.

Continue on.
Bring your arousal up to 40% and then repeat the process…one handholding your lingam, draw up the PC muscle, sweeping other hand to your heart with your breath, let go of tension both of the mind and body.

Allow the energy of you arousal to subside to 20%. You continue with self pleasuring while breathing deeply and rhythmically.
Can you move the energy with each breath, drawing it out of the lingam and into your heart?

You want to do this about 5 times, build the energy and then let it diffuse.

Know that between 70-100% (orgasm and ejaculation) happens really fast so you want to stop a couple of times when you are around 70% to your arousal capacity.

Feel the sensation through your whole body…allow the out breath to feel like a waterfall, pouring your energy down your whole body.

From here you might choose to bring yourself to ejaculation, but I would also encourage you to try not coming, teach the mind and body new tricks, they say this is the way to keep young.

In the Tantric belief system, your seminal fluid is your life force energy, if you can retain your essence it will build within you and you will be able to share this with your partner. She will absorb your yang essence from your lingam, the longer you can arouse her, the more yin essence she will have to share with you, which you absorb form her yoni.

The yin and yang of it, a deeply powerful way of balancing the Shiva and Shakti energies.

This exercise is not about whether you come or not, but about having the choice to decide when you want to. There may be much to unlearn within this process, go gently and with awareness. Recognise the habitual tensions of your body as you approach ejaculation. If you can recognise them and let them go now as you practice self pleasuring, then when you make love with your partner you will know the tensions and be able to let them go more easily.

Become aware of the tension as it builds, and then learn to do the opposite.

If you can direct the energy to your heart, then try to bring it up to the crown of your head, then combining it with the micro cosmic orbit.

Most of all enjoy.

Pleasure for the sake of pleasure; with no need to be anywhere other than the moment.

Begin to experiment with ejaculating 1 out of every 3 times, play around with it. It's not so much about not ejaculating; it's about being able to choose when you do.

The male orgasm occurs before ejaculation, so it is possible to orgasm and not ejaculate, known as a valley orgasm.

Tantra is about expanding awareness. See what happens, the places you can go within your own experience. Notice the minds story, can you let it go?

As you can probably see, this same technique can be used when making love. As you learn to stay present and connected to your sensations on your own, it will allow you to be present with both your sensations and hers when you come to making love.

You may get yourself to a point where you can injaculate, which is to orgasm without ejaculating.

You can't force yourself to meditate; it just doesn't work that way. I once heard it said that meditation happens by accident, but practice makes one accident prone.

So it is with the valley orgasm.

Only with time, awareness, patience and practice will this unfold for you.

Take your time, slow down, let go of expectation,
of striving to be anywhere other than where you are.
Be in the moment with a beginner's mind observing.
The awareness and observation is the Shiva element, the
ecstasy is the Shakti. Can you balance the two within
your own being?

How to know when she is ready.

The Taoist gave a precise prescription of how to read the stages of readiness in your woman.

As I stated earlier, the yin essence is cool and needs gentle warming. If a man tries to get into a woman's yin space too quickly, it generally creates a shut down. Remember, a man's heart is also yin and if a woman tries to get in there too quickly it also can lead to a shut down or out.

When we take the time to connect with our partner, we allow ourselves,

and our other, to be accepting of what is and resting within that, with no agenda, and no need to be anywhere other than where you both are in this moment.

The Taoists were very prescriptive as to how to read the signs of a woman's readiness.

As she tilts her head she is ready for you to touch her neck.

When she tilts her face to you, and her lips and eyes soften, she is ready to be kissed.

As she raises her breasts, then you will know they are ready to be touched.

When she arches her back, she is allowing and wanting, inviting the touch of her buttocks.

When her legs part, she is inviting the touch of her yoni and sacred jewel (clitoris).

When she is sufficiently wet and she arches her back, along with moans of pleasure, she is ready for you to enter her sacred temple.

There is no rushing this process, you need to allow each of the gates to open, to find the keys.

Personally, and from talking to many women, one of the most exquisite times of love making
occurs 'as the emperor is at the place gates'. Savour each moment, do not be in a hurry to enter, let her wanting draw you in.

Pleasure for the sake of pleasure.

Savour each sensual moment and then the next and the next.

Take your time; there is nowhere to be other than to be.

Let go of doing, come into being.

Let your love becomes a meditation, a prayer.

Watch your need for approval, your need to perform. It takes you away from being present with your beloved.

Communication

Find a language to explore.

Would you like me to…………………………?

Receiver responds with yes or no, thank you.

Giver; "Would you like it faster……slower……..harder……..softer?"

Giver say something positive such as "your skin feels so…….." "I love the way you surrender to my touch" "I love this feeling of connection………….you get the idea.

Non-violent Communication

When we can communicate our feelings and our needs, and ask for an action, we are much more likely to be heard and our needs met. This is very different from a demand.

'Can you hold me'….or 'Just hold me'.

OR

'I am feeling really vulnerable and what I need is to be held.
Would you please hold me in your arms?'

'Can you please slow down'…..or 'slow down'.

OR

'I am feeling really soft and in my feminine and what I need is for you to slow down'.

'I am trembling with pleasure, what I need is to stop and breathe with you for a moment.'

As the trust builds and we get more experienced in this way of communicating,

it may be that we can shorten the structure occasionally.

I need you to bite my neck

I need you to……………???

Sacral massage

Bringing energy to the sacrum will increase the energy and blood flow, and release blockages and tension. The sacrum is the triangular shaped bone at the spine, just above the coccyx.
The nerve and blood supply of the genitals wraps around and connects to the sacrum. The Kundalini energy, (sexual energy, life force energy, spiritual energy) lies dormant around the sacrum,
by massaging it we help to awaken this energy.

Rub your hands together and begin with circular movements to this area.
Use your thumbs and press over the top of the sacrum moving out towards the outer hips.
Using the heel of your hand, massage into the gluts, the fleshy butt cheeks.
Ask your partner if she/he would like it faster/slower, harder/softer.
Take your time, enjoy the process.
Give up in order to get somewhere.

Sensual massage

The idea of a sensual massage is to awaken sensation and build connection.

Combine breath with sensual touch.

Using gentle sensual circular movements, begin on the arms then move to the shoulders, chest, back, belly, from lower legs to upper. Move slowly, you are increasing sensate awareness.

Breathe together.

Read the signs of you partner as to when he/she is ready for you to touch the genitals and then ask her.

Go with awareness. You are massaging, which may get erotic but give up the mind's desire to go anywhere other than where you are lead moment by moment.

Breathe together.

Learn new and sensual ways to pleasure your partner. There is no prescription as to how every person likes to be touched, as everyone is different so you need to ask and communicate your wants, likes and desires.

Experiment with different stokes, ask your partner how he/she feels,

if he/she would like it faster/slower, softer/harder.

As the energy builds use the PC muscle with the inhalation to draw the energy up to your heart and into your whole body.

The masseuse can aid the movement of energy by sweeping a hand gently from yoni/lingam up to the heart. Feel the sensation through your whole body, allow the out breath to feel like a waterfall, pouring your energy into your whole body.

It is rarely that we touch our own or another's genitals unless for sexual gratification. Can you touch your lover all over with the same care, love, attention and devotion letting go of any need to get somewhere.

The Thrust of the matter.

Just as we have reflexology points all over the sole of our feet, the yoni and lingam have their own reflexology points.

With awareness you may begin to discover dull areas, or highly sensitive areas that are activated through touch. Emotions may be locked here, but with space, love and trust may be released.

When we thrust and thrust and thrust away, we can become desensitised.. This may hinder us from being able to fully open and surrender to the depths of our own pleasure capacity and that of our partners.

At the very tip of the lingam and the top of the yoni at the cervix,

we connect to our heart reflexology point.

Play around with different thrusting techniques, 4 shallow, 1 deep, or 5 shallow, 2 deep. Notice how this builds greater energy, she begins to want you more, drawing you deeper into her. If it is all deep thrusting, part of her and you may close down.

Find a rhythm, stick with that awhile and then mix it up.

The art is not in how Tantric a position is, but how Tantrically you fuck in any position. This means you are breathing...your attention is focused on your intention... and you are present in the moment and are not focusing on some future orgasmic goal.

Barbara Carrellas,
Urban Tantra: Sacred Sex for the Twenty-first Century.

Five Languages of Love. How does your cup get filled?

5 languages of love

by

Gary Chapman

The notion that we each get our cup of love filled in certain ways. One of the ways of feeling loved, of having your cup filled may stand out for you above the others, and it may be that another doesn't resonate at all with your needs.

Knowing what you need to have your cup filled allows you to communicate this to your partner. Usually the way that we get our cup filled, we presume that our beloved will be the same, which as you may imagine can lead to all sorts of miscommunication and misguided intention. For instance one of my partners from long ago felt his cup filled through acts of service,
so he would be forever fixing things, like my car. My primary way of feeling loved is through sharing quality time. So there he was actually removing himself from spending quality time by going out and fixing my car. I was not able to fully appreciate him fixing my car because I wanted to spend quality time ………and around and around we went.

Think about these different ways that we may each feel loved. Find out what yours is; it may not be just one thing, and communicate this with your partner.

1. Words of affirmation or appreciation.
2. Quality time
3. Receiving gifts
4. Acts of service.
5. Physical touch.

Your erotic persona.

Who are you in your love/ sensual realm?

When we step into this other realm, our sacred space, we shed the outer skin, we become vulnerable, we become real. We allow our beloved to see us for who we really are, beyond our job description, our marriage title, our daily struggles and disagreements. It may be that whoever you bring to your love space has a different persona.

Allow yourself the space to explore who you are, what you bring to you sensual/erotic love space. To drop the external persona and enter your ritual love space.

For instance, in everyday life you may be a very controlled or controlling person and your 'bedroom' persona actually wants to let go of control. Your need maybe for your beloved to take the reins so to speak, to be more in control sexually .

This may require some discussion and negotiation because chances are your partner may not see you at all in this way if your outer persona does not match. Is there something, an object or image that you can bring to the alter, or your bedroom space, that signifies this? This can be particularly helpful if you find it difficult to take off your outside hat and gloves. It may help you to connect with your ritual self and give permission to explore this aspect of you.

Create your own Tantric temple; however that looks and feels for you. Our relationships and the depth of our connections is what sustains and nourishes us. If you are single, you can explore a deeper sense of you, bringing a richness and wholeness to your life and the life of future possible relationships. If you are in a partnership, through this exploration, you are able to bring this deeper expression of you, your sensuality and sexuality to the mix.

Through Tantra we are able to find a more complete expression of us as sensual, erotic beings. We may find healing through trust and intimacy. We may deepen our connections and commitments to each other, or we may learn what it is, or who it is, we truly desire in our lives. For me, Tantra provides the playground, the garden of Eden where we may play, explore, dance, rest, eat and fully enjoy ourselves on all levels within.

Namaste.

Waratah Karleu

Waratah has taught yoga, mindfulness and wellness practices to children, teenagers and adults for over 20 years. She is a qualified Counsellor, Wellness Coach and Tantra Teacher, and is currently completing Masters studies in Sexology. Having a life long passion in maximising human potential and relationships, she believes the way forward is also about borrowing ancient knowledge from the past traditions of Yoga, Buddhist Mindfulness practices, Chinese Taoism and the Indian Tantric lineage.

In addition to studies, life has provided Waratah with many learnings and insights. Having traversed 15 years of marriage, which included the traumatic birth of her now 18 year old daughter and the subsequent physical and emotional healing beyond. The negotiating and renegotiating of affairs, open relationships, the breaking apart and coming back together of her marriage and the juggling of life, love and child rearing alongside the running of multiple businesses. All of which has granted a depth of lived experience to draw upon within her work as a therapist.

Waratah consults privately in person or via Skype and holds workshops in Australia and around the globe.

www.tantraadelaide.com